anythink.

BEYOND THE THEORY: SCIENCE OF THE FUTURE

DO PARALLEL UNIVERSES EXIST?

THEORIES ABOUT THE NATURE OF REALITY

Tom Jackson

 Gareth Stevens
PUBLISHING

Please visit our website, www.garethstevens.com.
For a free color catalog of all our high-quality books,
call toll free 1-800-542-2595 or fax 1-877-542-2596.

Cataloging-in-Publication Data

Names: Jackson, Tom.
Title: Do parallel universes exist? theories about the nature of reality / Tom Jackson.
Description: New York : Gareth Stevens Publishing, 2019. | Series: Beyond the theory: science of the future |
Includes glossary and index.
Identifiers: LCCN ISBN 9781538226650 (pbk.) | ISBN 9781538226643 (library bound)
Subjects: LCSH: Physics--Juvenile literature. | Quantum theory--Juvenile literature. |
General relativity (Physics)--Juvenile literature.
Classification: LCC QC25.J33 2019 | DDC 530--dc23

First Edition

Published in 2019 by
Gareth Stevens Publishing
111 East 14th Street, Suite 349
New York, NY 10003

© 2019 Gareth Stevens Publishing

Produced for Gareth Stevens by Calcium
Editors: Sarah Eason and Tim Cooke
Designers: Emma DeBanks and Lynne Lennon
Picture researcher: Rachel Blount

Picture credits: Cover: Shutterstock: GiroScience; Inside: Library of Congress: George Grantham Bain
Collection: p. 34; NASA: NASA/JPL/Cornell: p. 37; Shutterstock: Ge Amonthep: p. 15; Blend Images: p. 6;
Bo1982: p. 9; Color Chaser: p. 4; Hung Chung Chih: p. 5; Design Legendary: p. 21; Franz12: p. 40; Bianca
Grueneberg: p. 12; Lijuan Guo: p. 20; Viktor Hahn: p. 35; Happy Monkey: p. 10; Imagewriter: p. 8; IvanRiver:
p. 36; Maradon 333: p. 14; Anon Muenprom: p. 25; Parinya: p. 22; PeterPhoto123: p. 41; Anastasija Popova:
p. 16; Eduardo Rivero: p. 13; Sakkmesterk: pp. 1, 31, 33, 42; Olga Salt: p. 28; Sayasouk: p. 7; Yurchanka Siarhei:
p. 23; Studio Grand Ouest: p. 11; Taweepat: p. 38; Vchal: p. 32; Yakobchuk Viacheslav: p. 39; Vlue: p. 43;
Wikimedia Commons: pp. 18, 24; David Beck: p. 19; Chris Danals, National Science Foundation: p. 27; NASA/
JPL-Caltech: p. 30; NASA/JPL-Caltech/University of Wisconsin: p. 29; NASA/WMAP Science Team: p. 26;
Marie-Lan Nguyen (2011): p. 17.

Printed in the United States of America

CPSIA compliance information: Batch #CS18GS:
For further information contact Gareth Stevens, New York, New York at 1-800-542-2595.

CONTENTS

CHAPTER 1

INSIDE AND OUTSIDE

It might seem easy to define the universe. The universe is everything. But what is everything? Is it just what we can measure and detect—things like stars, **galaxies**, and planets? Or does it also include the contents of our heads—the stuff we remember, imagine, and dream?

The universe might include both what is around us and what is inside us.

4

Defining the universe is highly complicated. How do we explain the nature of space and how the universe formed? And how is the universe different from our **consciousness**? Consciousness makes us aware of the universe around us but also aware that we are looking at it. Is it possible to separate the universe outside us from the ideas we have about it in our heads?

This difference between external and internal universes suggests that there are many possible forms of a parallel universe or universes. A parallel universe is one that exists alongside our own. The word *universe* is based on a Latin phrase meaning "everything all around us." However, if parallel universes exist, then the universe cannot be everything. It must be just a part—even if it is a very big part—of everything. Instead of using the word universe, scientists tend to use the word multiverse, which means "many universes."

If parallel universes do exist, where does our universe end and the next one start? There are several possible answers, but they all have one thing in common. It is impossible to move from one universe to the next. That means we will never be able to find out anything about our neighboring universes—even whether they exist. In the end, perhaps parallel universes can only ever be ideas in our heads. To find out more, we have to go beyond the theory.

ALL IN THE MIND

Thinking about the universe—in other words, thinking about everything—starts inside your head. Everything you **perceive**, or are aware of, is formed within your brain. The brain tells you that some of those things—this book, your room, the stars—are outside your body in the rest of the universe. But you're also aware of other things inside you, such as memories, ideas, and emotions. Putting that all together, you create your own personal model of the universe (your little bit of it, anyway) inside your brain.

A child's idea of their universe might be very different from the ideas of their friends or parents.

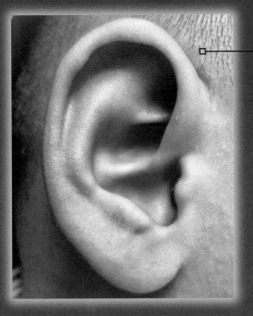

The ear is one of the main ways we get information about the world. Its tiny hairs sense changes in the air.

That model is built from information streaming into the brain from your **senses**. People often talk about the five senses, but our bodies contain dozens of sensory systems. The first four are obvious. The eyes are used for vision, which builds a picture of what is around you from light reflecting off objects. The nose and tongue detect chemicals in the air and in our food, creating sensations of smell and taste. The ears are for hearing, picking up changes in air pressure caused by motion around you. The "fifth" sense is touch—and this is where things gets messy. The ear is a touch organ—it feels minute vibrations in the air. However, the ear also contains the balance organs, which tell the brain how the body is moving. The skin picks up bigger pressure changes, which we call "touch"—but it is also detecting hot and cold, wet and dry, and works with the muscles to tell the brain what shape the body is making.

UNANSWERED

Vast amounts of sensory information flood into the brain every second, but we are not aware of it all. Instead, the brain presents only the important information to give you your own personal version of reality. Everyone's version of reality is different, and it is difficult to know whether another person's version is the same as our own. However, there is a way of matching up everyone's versions of reality to reveal the truth about the universe. It is called science.

WHICH REALITY?

Reality is another word like universe. At first, it seems easy to understand. It simply means "everything that is real." The more you think about the idea of reality, however, you find that there is more than one kind of "real."

Most people divide reality in two: one reality outside us and another that exists inside our minds. These are called objective reality and subjective reality, respectively. Objective reality is information that comes from outside the body—the sights, sounds, and smells of objects. Subjective reality is created inside the mind. Our **perceptions** of it are subject to emotions and memories. To put it simply, objective reality deals with facts while subjective reality is concerned with ideas. However, that leads to more complications. How can you tell the difference between the two? In general it is obvious which is which. However, we are easily fooled.

A white vase or two black silhouettes? Our brain can be quite easily fooled by **optical illusions**.

When it comes to discovering new facts, we follow a system to ensure our senses are not being fooled. This system is called the scientific method. It divides objective fact from subjective thoughts.

BEHIND ᴛʜᴇ THEORY

The scientific method was developed over centuries, but the first person to write it out as a clear system was the English lawyer Francis Bacon. Bacon, who worked for the English royal family in the seventeenth century, was interested in all kinds of knowledge. For example, he wanted to know why keeping food cold kept it fresh. During a snowstorm in 1626, Bacon bought a chicken and stuffed it with snow. He got so cold that he died from pneumonia two weeks later. The chicken lasted longer than Bacon did.

The scientific method can be broken down into a series of six steps:

Step 1: Observe nature.
Step 2: Ask a question about how nature works.
Step 3: Come up with the answer you think is correct. This is called the **hypothesis**.
Step 4: Test the hypothesis. To do this you will need to construct an experiment and predict its results. If the hypothesis is correct, then the predicted result will be the one you get.
Step 5: If the hypothesis is true, it becomes a **theorem**. How does the theorem change the way we understand objective nature?
Step 6: Ask another question.

Laboratory research is based on observation and experimentation.

THEORY OF MIND

Only humans perform scientific experiments. At least, as far as we know. Perhaps dogs are performing a huge experiment on their human owners? It is unlikely, but it is impossible to say for sure that they are not. One of the limits of the scientific method is that it cannot prove a negative idea, such as that animals are not doing science. The method could show us if they are, but without any evidence, we have to assume that they are not.

The best evidence that humans are the only scientific creatures in the world is called the theory of mind. However, "mind" is another tricky word to define.

There is a chance that dogs—and kittens—are doing their own form of science, but it is highly unlikely.

UNANSWERED

We develop a theory of mind around the age of three or four. That is why children of that age love to play hide and seek. Players have to understand that the seeker does not know where they are—even though the hider knows. The theory of mind is crucial to help us start separating facts about reality from our thoughts and dreams. However, it also shows that we all live in our own parallel universes, separate from everyone else's.

We use it in many ways, but in the theory of mind, the word "mind" describes the collection of internal images, words, and feelings that make up a person's thoughts. The mind is created by the brain, but it feels to us like a separate thing. The theory of mind is the realization that what is in your mind is different from what is in someone else's. You can tell people what is in your mind—through language, music, or math, for example—but they cannot experience your thoughts as you do.

Very young children often think they can hide by simply covering their own eyes.

CHAPTER 2

INTERNAL WORLDS

There is no doubt that humans are highly intelligent animals. Our intelligence has allowed us to examine and learn much about the structure and history of the universe. That includes everything from the life cycle of stars to the origins of humans themselves. Oddly, one of the things that makes us so smart is that we all live in our own little worlds—and that gets us thinking.

Human intelligence comes from figuring out what might happen in the future and then making a plan. The human mind can imagine the future as well as remember the past, which means we have ideas about what is the best thing to do next. For example, our ancestors prepared for winter by storing food. They saw rain clouds and set out bowls to collect rainwater to drink.

It is only when someone can imagine the future that they can collect rainwater.

Evidence shows that, around 50,000 years ago, our ancestors started having good ideas much more often. They invented new technologies and learned to survive in new regions. This so-called Great Leap Forward may have been when our ancestors started using complex language to share their ideas—and working together to have better ones.

Philosophers have wondered about how the mind relates to the universe. One way to look at it is that the whole universe is contained in your head. Only the mind truly exists, and the external world is formed inside the mind. This idea is called solipsism, and its most extreme form is that only one mind exists—your own. Everything in the universe, including everyone else (and their ideas) are all made up inside your head. A less lonely version says that other minds exist—yours and everyone else's—but they are cut off from one another. So every mind is in effect its own parallel universe.

Cave paintings and ancient tools are evidence of a great technological advance about 50,000 years ago.

DREAMS

The universe has laws that govern things such as **gravity**, light, magnetism, and electricity. These are examples of objective facts, which we all agree are real. We can never escape them. Wherever we go in our universe, the laws always apply—that is one of the laws. However, every night we can leave this universe and visit a parallel one where the rules have all changed. In this other universe, we can fly, visit with dead relatives, and go to new worlds. We just need to dream.

As we sleep, our body follows a routine called the sleep cycle. The sleep cycle sees the body getting more relaxed over a 90-minute period, being less and less aware of what is going on around it. Each sleep cycle ends with a stage called REM, or rapid eye movement.

Dreams often assemble random episodes into sequences that seem to relate to one another.

UNANSWERED

Dreaming is a mystery. Why does it happen? It seems to be something the brain has to do now and again. While the body is relaxed and inactive during sleep, the brain is busy. One suggestion is that it is processing what has happened in the day, figuring out what to remember and what to forget. To do that, the brain needs to tell itself a story, which is the dream. The story may relate to past memories, people we know, or our worries and fears. Or it might just be nonsense made out of unconnected brain activity.

The muscles stay paralyzed, but your eyes roll behind the lids and the brain appears to wake up inside the sleeping body. This is a dream. It may be an exciting adventure in which you are a superhero, a scary nightmare filled with monsters—or a normal(ish) set of events. We have about five REM stages of sleep each night. Each lasts only a few minutes, and each produces a new dream. Everyone has dreams, but some people cannot remember them when they wake up. For others, dreams make up a large part of their experiences.

Everyone dreams from an early age.

CHAPTER 3

CONSCIOUSNESS

The mind, dreams, imagination, and intelligence: these are all parts of an important idea called consciousness. Humans are—or at least think they are—conscious beings. Consciousness is what makes us aware of the universe and allows us to explore its complexities with science and philosophy. At its heart, consciousness is based on a sense of self. A conscious being—like you—is aware that they are separate from the rest of the universe and in charge of their own actions.

So far, the riddles of consciousness have not been solved by science. No one is sure what it is, where it comes from, or whether it is unique to humans. Could it be that animals, or even plants, are conscious of themselves?

No one knows if an animal such as a horse is conscious of itself.

Greek doctors first figured out the role of the brain.

Does consciousness mean that, while humans are able to express the contents of our minds through language, math, and art, we cannot communicate with cats and trees in the same way, even though they are conscious in their own way? Or is consciousness a new thing that only really appeared in humans? And how has consciousness evolved from ancient peoples to humans today?

The ancient Egyptians thought that the brain was a system for cooling the blood. They believed that their actions and desires were controlled not by the brain but by the heart. People today still talk about the heart in relation to our most powerful emotions, such as love and hate.

Greek doctors, such as Galen in the early third century AD, and Arab scholars, such as Avicenna in the eleventh century, were responsible for shifting our attention to the brain. Avicenna thought the brain was filled with liquid spirits, which merged all the information from the different senses into a "common sense" at the heart of the brain, which is where we made decisions. Modern neuroscience—the study of the brain—has discovered a lot more about how the brain actually works. It is based not on liquid spirits but on pulses between **nerve** ends. However, neuroscience has produced just as many questions about consciousness as answers. Let's think about that.

I THINK
THEREFORE I AM

One of the most famous philosophical sayings is "I think, therefore I am." It means that because you are able to think about whether you exist, you must exist. The man who said it was René Descartes, a seventeenth-century French philosopher and mathematician. Descartes' observation started with a dream.

RENATVS CARTESIVS.

Descartes was a sickly child, and his teachers let him do school work in bed. As an adult, too, Descartes often worked in bed. One morning in the 1630s, Descartes awoke and began his day, only to suddenly wake up all over again. The start of his day had been a dream!

Descartes' theory is one of the foundations of all philosophy.

Descartes was baffled. How could he know if he was awake now, or still asleep? He concluded that if he were dreaming he would not be questioning whether he was awake. Since he was doubting he was awake, he must be awake. That idea extends to consciousness. Something becomes conscious once it begins to wonder if it is conscious or whether its perceptions are an illusion. If the mind were an illusion, Descartes decided, it would not be aware that it might be an illusion!

As well as explaining consciousness and existence, René Descartes also invented graphs. It was his idea to turn mathematical relationships into lines plotted against vertical and horizontal axes—and turning plotted lines into equations. Descartes worked as a teacher for Europe's royalty. His last job was for Queen Christina in Sweden. Christina wanted lessons at 5:00 A.M., and her castle was very cold. Descartes soon became sick and died.

Queen Christina's study habits were too much for Descartes.

Descartes described the conscious mind not as part of the physical body but as a spirit that was beyond scientific observation. He saw the body as a flesh robot that sent information to the pineal gland, a tiny part of the brain. This gland interacted with the mind, and then communicated instructions back to the body by spreading vibrations through the body. The actual link between the brain and the body is better understood today. However, there is still something about consciousness that seems to be separate from the body. That is why we cannot share each other's experiences.

HARD PROBLEMS

Neuroscience has come a long way since the time of Descartes. However, while scientists have figured out how the brain and body are connected, there are still some hard problems of consciousness that have not been solved by science.

Imagine a zombie that has nerves, a brain, muscles, senses—but no conscious mind. It looks and behaves like a regular person. You know the zombie is not conscious, but there is no test to prove it. Even cutting him open (it's okay, he's a zombie!) would not reveal any differences between his brain and yours. So what is the difference that makes you conscious? It is all the sensations of experience, such as the taste of ice cream, the sound of music, and the colors of the rainbow. These sensations are known as **qualia**. The brain is active when we experience qualia—and yet the experiences do not exist in the brain.

How each of us experiences the seven colors in a rainbow may be very different.

Zombies have no consciousness— yet their brains would appear identical to those of people who do have consciousness.

The experiences exist somewhere else. It is impossible to compare the qualia in one mind with the qualia in another mind. Your experience of blue may not match the blue qualia in another mind.

So although he was not right about how the body worked, Descartes was still correct. The conscious mind and the body appear to be separate. That is, if consciousness is even real in the first place!

UNANSWERED

A zombie is a dead body that has come back to life. The idea comes from voodoo, a religion from the Caribbean and South America. Whether it has ever happened, we will never know. Some traditional voodoo potions contain pufferfish. The fish has a poison that makes the heart beat so slowly, someone who took it might appear dead. Once the poison wears off, the heart recovers—and the person comes "back from the dead"!

LIVING IN THE PAST

The brain is an electrical organ. It contains 83 billion nerve cells that send signals between one another using electric pulses. Neuroscientists have studied the electrical activity of the brain to see if they could figure out which part of the brain was making the decisions. What they discovered suggested that we are not really in charge of ourselves at all!

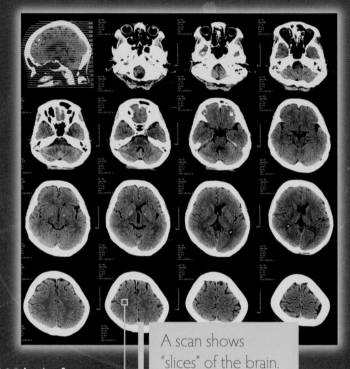

A scan shows "slices" of the brain. Scientists are trying to figure out what parts of the brain are responsible for different functions.

The body contains nearly 60 miles (100 km) of nerves. These fibers carry signals in two directions. Sensory nerves carry information from the body and the senses to the brain. Motor nerves send instructions from the brain to the muscles. The information is handled by the sensory and motor **cortices**, which are regions at the top of the brain. When someone decides to make a movement, a region called the premotor cortex sends an electrical signal to a brain region called the motor cortex and out to the body.

UNANSWERED

Tests on the premotor cortex suggest we are not making conscious decisions about our bodies, so we are not fully in charge of them. That means we do not have what philosophers call **free will**. But we may have "free won't." In other words, it is not the job of our consciousness to control every aspect of our behavior. That happens automatically. Instead, our consciousness watches and inhibits, or stops, any actions that seem like a bad idea.

The brain has four major distinct areas, called lobes.

In the 1980s, brain researchers used new brain scanners to study this process. In tests, however, they found that the premotor cortex turned on a third of a second before the test subject decided to make a movement. This suggests that people do not actually decide to make movements—the movements happen automatically. We feel that we are deciding, but that is not the same.

Although some scientists are not convinced by the results of these tests, this could mean that our responses to events are always slightly behind real time. Does the same apply to our awareness of those events? That would mean our consciousness is more like an instant replay, playing back just after the real thing has happened. The decisions that control our body are made in the gap between the real time and the replay.

CHAPTER 4

BIG PICTURE

The scientific method may not be able to solve the hardest problems of consciousness, but it has helped us figure out the structure of the universe. The study of the universe and its formation is called cosmology. Thanks to cosmologists, our understanding of the universe keeps getting bigger.

Less than 500 years ago, most people believed Earth was at the center of the universe, cut off from the heavens by a ring of fire. Beyond the ring of fire, the moon, sun, and five planets—not eight—**orbited** Earth. The stars were fixed lights on the inside of a crystal sphere that formed the edge of the universe.

This engraving from 1888 shows a traveler breaking through the crystal sphere surrounding the medieval universe.

This idea of the universe dates from the time of the ancient Greek philosopher Aristotle in the fourth century BC. Early Christian thinkers said that the universe was perfect and could not change.

On May 24, 1543, the Polish astronomer Nicolaus Copernicus changed all that. He put the sun at the center of the universe, with Earth and the other planets in orbit around it. However, since then more discoveries have moved Earth farther and farther from the center of the universe. We now know that our sun is near the edge of a galaxy called the Milky Way, which contains billions of suns. The Milky Way is one of billions of galaxies in the universe, and each of these galaxies has billions more stars and trillions of planets—some of which are probably very similar to our own.

These discoveries are in line with an idea called the Copernican principle, named for Copernicus. The Copernican principle says that Earth and its human inhabitants do not occupy a special place in the universe. In fact, as astronomers and other scientists try to figure out where our universe comes from, they have discovered that it is possible that even the universe itself does not have a special place. It may be one of many—perhaps an **infinity**—of parallel universes. That is a shocking thought. Let's see where it comes from.

OUT OF REACH

A century ago astronomers not only discovered that the universe is much bigger than they had originally thought. They also realized it is getting bigger all the time—fast. If the universe will be bigger tomorrow, they figured, then it must have been smaller yesterday. That must mean that, if we went far enough back in time, the universe—the whole thing—would be a tiny dot. This idea led to the best theory cosmologists have of how the universe started.

The theory is called the Big Bang. Lots of evidence supports the theory, but there is still one thing scientists cannot explain. Wherever they look with powerful telescopes, the universe looks the same. **Matter** and energy are spread out evenly. The size of the universe suggests they would be more uneven. Scientists think the universe must have expanded very quickly in the first instant of its existence, which locked in the smoothness.

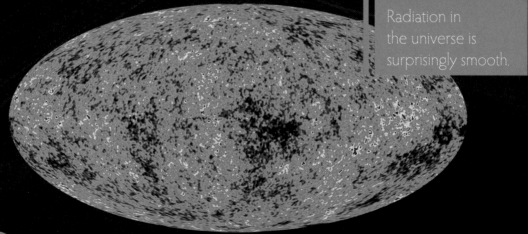

Radiation in the universe is surprisingly smooth.

BEHIND THE THEORY

The theory of cosmic inflation was put together by an American physicist named Alan Guth in 1979. Guth then spent the next 35 years looking for evidence that the theory is true. In 2014, the BICEP2 detector at the South Pole found electrical ripples in deep space. Some scientists believe they are caused by cosmic **inflation**, so they prove that Guth is right. However, other scientists say the results need more analysis.

This process, called cosmic inflation, made the universe expand faster than the speed of light. Although nothing can move through space faster than light, space itself can grow faster than light. Light travels through space at a fixed speed of one light-year in a year. The universe is 13.8 billion years old, and we can only see light from objects that are less than 13.8 billion light-years away. Due to inflation, most of the universe is farther away from us than that. We can never see it because it is getting farther away from us faster than the speed of light. The definition of a parallel universe is space that we can never observe. In that case, our universe is surrounded by a parallel universe—at least one. There may be many more.

The BICEP2 detector at the South Pole studies electrical ripples in space.

BUBBLE UNIVERSES

In theory, our universe is just one of many.

The way cosmic inflation works suggests that it is a process that never ends. That would mean that our universe is just one bubble of space among an infinity of parallel universes.

According to the theory of cosmic inflation, when the universe was created, it was very small and very hot. As it cooled, all the forces that make the universe work began to appear. These included forces such as electricity and magnetism. At the beginning of the universe, however, all the forces were merged into one. That force created the outward force that pushed the universe apart.

The material that created this negative gravity is highly unstable and breaks down easily. During its inflation, our universe doubled in size at least 100 times in only 10^{-35} seconds (that's 0.0 with 34 more 0s followed by a 1). In that time, it went from the size of a **subatomic particle** called a **proton** to about the size of a marble. After that time, inflation stopped. From then on, the universe grew according to the regular laws of **physics**.

However, it was only the first marble-sized bubble of space that stopped inflating. The space around it kept going. Bubble universes popped up whenever their patch of space broke down into regular matter and energy.

As far as scientists know, the process is still going on, with tiny new universes being formed all the time. And the process will go on forever. Not all these bubble universes are alike. Among an infinite number of universes, there will be every conceivable version of the universe. That includes a version out there somewhere that is identical to our own universe—complete with an identical version of you!

Could bubbles in distant galaxies be signs of alternative universes?

UNANSWERED

The universe is full of opposites that work against each other, such as **mass** and gravity. If you add together all the mass and gravity energy in the universe, the total is zero. That suggests the universe could have come from nothing. In that case, what set off the Big Bang? Perhaps it was an older universe bubble bursting, splitting in two, or colliding with a neighbor. Or perhaps our bubble universe is young compared to others in a multiverse that has no beginning and no end.

DARK
MATTER.

Most of the universe is missing. Scientists have figured out that 86 percent of the universe's mass is nowhere to be seen. Is this evidence of a parallel universe in another dimension?

In the 1930s, astronomers began measuring how much mass was in galaxies using the light coming from stars. They also measured how fast galaxies spin. They found that galaxies were spinning too fast for their mass. They should be flinging out stars in all directions, like a galactic garden sprinkler. The fact that they do not means there is matter giving mass to galaxies that we cannot see. This is dark matter.

This illustration imagines dark matter as rays in space.

Dark matter does not produce light, which means it is also not affected by electricity or magnetism. Dark matter moves through ordinary matter as if it was not there. It is streaming through your body right now. The only thing dark matter does do is make gravity.

BEHIND THE THEORY

We experience three dimensions of space. Higher spatial dimensions may hold parallel universes, but we are unable to see them. This idea is illustrated in *Flatland*, an 1884 book by Edwin Abbott Abbott. It was a story about a civilization with two dimensions where everyone is a flat shape. One day a three-dimensional character, Sphere, arrives. Flatland's walls are lines and Sphere can jump them by moving up in the third dimension. Flatlanders could not see up or down, so to them Sphere disappeared and then reappeared on the other side of the wall!

One theory is that dark matter is formed by mass from nearby parallel universes. No light comes from these universes because light only travels through space, and their space is separate from ours. But the mass of these universes bends our space, creating the effects of gravity. If this idea is true, our neighboring universes occupy **hyperspace**. In other words, they use different dimensions of space—the fourth dimension and beyond.

The mass of other universes may be bending space in our universe.

CHAPTER 5

THE QUANTUM WORLD

Cosmology creates a big picture of our universe that gives us some ideas about parallel universes. However, science also looks at the smallest things in nature. Quantum physics is the study of atoms and subatomic particles. It has its own ideas about parallel universes.

Quantum physics is interested in what is going on inside atoms. Atoms are the smallest particles that can exist of a particular substance, such as gold or oxygen. Atoms of different substances are different, but all atoms are made of various combinations of smaller subatomic particles. The outer region of an atom is filled with **electrons**. These are negatively charged particles that barely have any mass, or weight, at all.

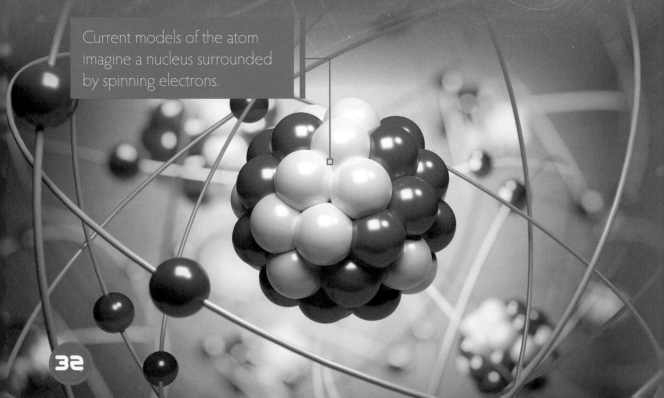

Current models of the atom imagine a nucleus surrounded by spinning electrons.

This computer-generated image imagines pieces of energy being released by tiny particles.

Most of the mass of an atom is in the nucleus. This is a dense core made up of protons and neutrons. Protons have a positive charge that pulls on the negative charge of the electrons, holding them in place. Neutrons have no charge. However, the story does not end there. Protons and neutrons are made from three electron-sized particles called quarks. The quarks are held together by a force known as the **strong force**. This is by far the strongest force in the universe. The energy used to keep quarks together is what gives protons, neutrons, nuclei, atoms, and everything else mass, or weight.

The quantum in quantum physics refers to energy. Energy does not flow in and out of subatomic particles like a liquid. It travels in very precise quantities, known as quanta. Adding a quantum of energy to an electron, for example, alters its characteristics, such as the way it spins or its position in an atom. However, at this scale it is not possible to measure these characteristics. Instead, quantum physicists calculate how probable it is that a particle has a certain set of states. This uncertainty makes quantum physics very weird. One view of it suggests that every time a quantum of energy moves from one particle to the next, it creates a new set of parallel universes. (How's that for weird?)

MANY WORLDS

The facts of quantum physics are well understood, but their meaning is open to interpretation. The first interpretation of quantum physics was made in the 1920s. It is known as the Copenhagen Interpretation.

The Danish physicist Niels Bohr came up with the Copenhagen interpretation.

The Copenhagen Interpretation describes a particle using a type of mathematics called a wave function. The math shows all the possible states the particle could have, and the chances of each being correct. Until a particle is measured—we can only measure one of its characteristics at a time—no one knows which state is correct. In a wave function, the particle is in all those states at once, an idea called superposition. Superposition means an electron can be in two places at once. (In quantum physics, this is completely normal.) Once we measure the particle, the Copenhagen Interpretation says the wave function has "collapsed." The chance of the electron being in another location disappears. This idea allows us to explain how super-weird quantum particles make non-quantum processes work, including chemical reactions, starlight, the weather, and sounds.

BEHIND THE THEORY

The Austrian physicist Erwin Schrödinger demonstrated superposition with a famous idea called Schrödinger's Cat. A cat is in a closed box with a vial of poison. The poison is only released when some uranium decays, a quantum process that cannot be predicted. Schrödinger's point was that, until you look in the box to check, the cat is in superposition—it is both dead and alive. By extension, that means everything in the universe is also in superposition—a fuzzy mess of possibilities—until you look at it. Only then does the universe decide what state it is truly in.

Erwin Schrödinger imagined a cat in a box that was both dead and alive.

In 1957, the US physicist Hugh Everett came up with an interpretation of quantum physics called the Many-Worlds Interpretation (MWI). This idea does not use wave-function collapse. Instead, all of the possible states of a quantum particle enter alternative histories! A new set of histories appears every time particles exchange energy. If MWI is correct, there are a nearly infinite number of "worlds." That means there are parallel universes filled with versions of you with different histories. Every time you make a decision, there is another universe where you decided something else!

MEETING YOURSELF

Parallel universes offer the possibility—in fact, the certainty—that there is another version of you somewhere. In some cases they will be identical to you, with the same past and the same future. In other universes they look like you but have led a very different life. What would happen if you met yourself? Who would be who?

Philosophers have thought a lot about what gives a person an **identity**. Is it a collection of experiences gathered over a lifetime? Is it the drive for survival that ensures your mind is always linked to the body? We might find out the answer if we moved to a parallel universe. Let's imagine the Many-Worlds Interpretation is correct. In this multiverse, the history of your different selves is always different from your own. Your other versions have lived a different life from you and collected different experiences, so they have a different identity. They may look similar, but are more like a twin, not an exact copy.

Versions of yourself in a multiverse are like you—but not exactly the same.

BEHIND THE THEORY

In 1984, British philosopher Derek Parfit imagined being **teleported** to Mars. Something goes wrong and two versions of Derek appear on Mars. At the instant they appear, they have identical memories and bodies, but from that moment they live separate lives. Parfit used this thought experiment to suggest that a person's identity only exists right now. It is always changing. Just as there is no connection between the two Martian Dereks—just ideas they share—there is no connection between you yesterday and you tomorrow. You'll be different then!

Now let's visit a bubble universe caused by eternal cosmic inflation. Of our many choices, we go to one identical to our home universe. The version of you there is identical in every way. You both know the same things, and think the same way. Your brains and consciousness are identical, and you must be having the same thoughts. However, there is something different about you. You have traveled through hyperspace to visit the alternative universe, which would be something your parallel version has not done. Unless they did the same thing—in which case they are now in this universe looking for you!

Derek Parfit imagined two Dereks on Mars.

CHAPTER 6

MAKING REALITIES

Science is as much about creativity as it is about facts and experiments. To make new discoveries about the universe or the workings of the brain, scientists spend time dreaming up new ideas. Most of these ideas will never be tested, but they tell us something important. If we want to visit a parallel universe, we can just imagine one.

Famous stories such as *Star Wars*, *The Lord of the Rings*, and the *Harry Potter* series all take place in parallel universes. Some things about those places are familiar to us. The same laws of physics apply there (more or less).

In the imagination, it's possible to travel to a magical parallel universe just by getting on a train.

Virtual reality can make experiences that are impossible in our universe seem real to us.

However, these universes also possess phenomena that do not exist in our universe. We could call them magic, but we really mean they appear to break the laws of physics.

The rules of physics governing these imaginary parallel universes allow phenomena such as telepathy (reading someone else's mind) or telekinesis (moving objects without touching them). In that case, such phenomena are not really magic—just stuff that happens in other universes. These imaginary worlds have been made up inside someone's head, but according to the many-worlds theory and eternal cosmic inflation, the Death Star, Middle Earth, and Hogwarts are all really out there in the multiverse.

Our imaginations are limitless, but so is the multiverse. Is there a link between the two? In the multiverse, whatever you dream up, however strange, is sure to exist already. We can never actually visit, but we can go there in our minds. Many people have imagined ways of creating entire universes that we can all experience together. One way might be by improved virtual reality. A few people have even wondered if we are already living in virtual reality, only this time created by someone or something else. Just imagine that!

VIRTUAL REALITY

Virtual reality technology is a big trick. It is designed to convince the senses that you are in a different location from where you are. It might be another world or it might be our world, but seen from the size of an ant. It might even be experiencing our world by living inside the body of someone else.

The word "virtual" refers to something that appears to be real and can be measured and described in the ways we use for real things—but it is not real. The simplest example is a mirror image. It appears to be on the other side of the mirror. Step toward the mirror and the virtual image also gets closer. Stand back, and it moves away. However, there is nothing behind the mirror. The image is created by reflected light beams. Your brain turns the light into a mental picture that looks just as real as everything else.

Virtual reality creates its own universe by tricking the eyes with tiny pixels of light.

UNANSWERED

It is already possible to play games in virtual reality, and there are online communities populated with **avatars**—virtual people. Those avatars represent real people. When combined with VR, an avatar perceives other avatars as real people. This raises interesting questions about identity. Is an avatar representing a real person perceived by another avatar representing another real person therefore a real person? If you kill an avatar in VR, are you a murderer?

An avatar is a VR version of a real person. Does it have the same rights as a real person?

The idea of virtual reality (VR) is over 50 years old, but technology is only just catching up. A VR headset uses two small screens, one for each eye, to show a scene. The left scene is slightly different from the right one, which is how our eyes see reality. The brain turns the two images into a three-dimensional experience that looks real. Headphones add sound, and sensors track the movement of the head and body to alter the scene on screen to give the impression that the user is moving in space.

The human eye focuses on only a small part of a scene. The VR headset makes that spot sharp with the rest more blurred to provide a more real experience. Haptic, or touch, technology uses gloves to push on the fingertips when a user touches a virtual object, so they can "feel" it. Eventually, a virtual world could look and feel the same as the real one. VR will then take us to any parallel universe we can imagine.

IS REALITY A SIMULATION?

VR technology is a way to create a universe with its own set of rules. Cosmologists do something similar. They create simulated universes inside computers and run them at high speed, watching as the models develop. They fine-tune their rules to see what difference that makes to the end results. This helps them understand how the universe became the way it is.

The philosopher Nick Bostrom wondered if it might be possible that our universe is a simulation running on an alien computer. He figured it would take a very advanced civilization to produce such a complex simulated universe. He considered how likely it is that a civilization could become that advanced.

Could our universe be a simulation generated inside a computer in another universe?

BEHIND THE THEORY

Born in Sweden, Nick Bostrom now works in Oxford, England. He is an expert in thinking about the future. Among the subjects he studies are the ways in which we might alter our bodies or the bodies of other creatures in the future, and how artificial intelligence (AI) will change the world. Bostrom also speculates about whether humans are intelligent enough not to destroy our own planet in the future.

It would take a long time, during which wars, diseases, exploding suns, or **meteorite** impacts might halt progress. If a civilization was advanced enough to model a universe, would it bother? Bostrom concluded that the chances were very low. However, if just one civilization could model many universes—perhaps billions—there would be more simulated universes than real ones, maybe including ours.

Why would someone simulate a universe? Perhaps it is a version of reality TV. Perhaps alien children keep universes as pets! What do you think this universe is for? If we will never know about parallel universes, does it even matter whether or not they exist?

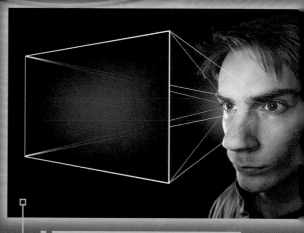

We know we can simulate other universes. That may mean other civilizations can do the same thing.

TIMELINE

Nicolaus Copernicus proposes that Earth and the other planets orbit the sun, rather than all the other heavenly bodies orbiting Earth, as previously believed.

English scholar Francis Bacon writes the first version of what is now called the scientific method.

René Descartes publishes his famous observation about consciousness, "I think, therefore I am."

English schoolteacher Edwin Abbott Abbott publishes the book *Flatland: A Romance in Many Dimensions*, which imagines a two-dimensional world.

George Lemaitre proposes a theory of the creation of the universe now known as the Big Bang Theory.

The Dane Niels Bohr and the German Werner Heisenberg come up with the Copenhagen Interpretation, which is an explanation of quantum physics.

US astronomer Edwin Hubble observes that the universe is constantly expanding.

Austrian physicist Erwin Schrödinger uses the story of Schrödinger's Cat to explain superposition in subatomic particles.

Swiss astrophysicist Fritz Zwicky proposes that much of the weight of galaxies is contained in "dark matter."

Inventors begin to create early types of virtual reality machines.

| 1957 | US physicist Hugh Everett comes up with the Many-Worlds Interpretation of quantum physics. |

US physicist Hugh Everett comes up with the Many-Worlds Interpretation of quantum physics.

US astronomer Vera Rubin observes the Andromeda galaxy and finds the first clear evidence of the existence of dark matter.

US astronomer Alan Guth proposes the theory of cosmic inflation to explain the early history of the universe.

Scientists begin to use advanced scanners to study the structure and workings of the brain.

British philosopher Derek Parfit proposes a thought experiment in which he is teleported to Mars, but arrives as two identical figures.

Swedish-born philosopher Nick Bostrom publishes a paper suggesting that we might be living inside the computer simulation of another civilization.

The BICEP2 observatory at the South Pole measures electrical ripples in deep space that might be the first confirmation of the cosmic inflation theory.

Facebook buys the virtual reality company Oculus VR for $2 billion. Oculus, Sony, Google, and more than 200 other companies are developing VR headsets and other technology.

GLOSSARY

atoms the smallest particles that can exist

avatars figures representing real people in video games or computer simulations

consciousness the state of being aware of oneself and one's surroundings

cortices (sing. cortex) the outer layers of the brain

dimension a measurable extent of a quality such as height or mass

electrons subatomic particles in the nuclei of atoms

free will the ability to decide one's own actions

galaxies systems of millions or billions of stars held together by gravity

gravity the force by which all physical bodies attract one another

hyperspace a space that has more than three dimensions that surrounds space as we are aware of it

hypothesis an explanation of something based on limited evidence

identity the characteristics that decide who or what a person is

infinity something that has no ending or beginning

inflation growing in all directions

mass the amount of matter something contains

matter the substance of which physical objects are made

meteorite a piece of rock or metal that falls to a planet from space

nerve a whitish fiber in the body that transmits signals to and from the brain

optical illusions visual tricks that fool the eyes

orbited followed a regular path around a star or other body in space

perceive to interpret something in a particular way

perceptions the ways in which something is regarded or understood

philosophers people who think about serious questions of existence

physics the science of matter and energy

proton a subatomic particle in the nucleus of an atom

qualia qualities of physical things as experienced by an individual person

quantum physics the branch of science that explains the behavior of atoms and subatomic particles

senses the ways in which the body experiences external things

strong force the force that holds atoms and particles together

subatomic particle a particle that is part of an atom

teleported traveled instantly across some distance of space

theorem a statement that is not proved but is supported by evidence

BOOKS

Edge, Christopher. *The Many Worlds of Albie Bright.* New York, NY: Delacorte Books for Young Readers, 2017.

Keranen, Rachel. *The Big Bang Theory.* New York, NY: Cavendish Square Publishing, 2017.

May, Brian. *Exploring the Mysteries of the Universe.* New York, NY: Rosen Young Adult, 2016.

Woodford, Chris, and Martin Clowes. *Atoms and Molecules: Investigating the Building Blocks of Matter.* New York, NY: Rosen Central, 2013.

WEBSITES

www.dkfindout.com/uk/space/stars-and-galaxies/big-bang
A Dorling Kindersley page about the creation of the universe in the Big Bang.

starchild.gsfc.nasa.gov/docs/StarChild/universe_level2/cosmology.html
A guide to cosmology from the Star Child project at NASA.

www.dummies.com/education/science/physics/the-theory-of-parallel-universes
A Dummies page that explains theories about parallel universes.

www.esa.int/esaKIDSen/SEM0V1BE8JG_OurUniverse_0.html
European Space Agency pages about the structure of the universe.

INDEX